LAST POEMS
BEFORE HEART FAILURE

TODD SWIFT

LAST POEMS BEFORE HEART FAILURE

BLACK SPRING SPECIAL PAMPHLET

THE **BLACK SPRING**
PRESS GROUP

○○○ MAIDA VALE PUBLISHING

First published in 2022
by Maida Vale Publishing Ltd
United Kingdom

Typeset with artwork and graphic design by Edwin Smet

ISBN 978-1-915406-02-6

BLACKSPRINGPRESSGROUP.COM

NOTE
this pamphlet consists of poems written in 2021 –
none have been previously published except in a few
instances on social media; any echoes of previous styles
or stylistic periods is intentional.

This book was written before the unprovoked
and despicable invasion of Ukraine in 2022.

For more information on Heart Failure (HF) please see:
https://www.bhf.org.uk/informationsupport/conditions/heart-failure

A SPECIAL THANK YOU TO
THE NURSES AND DOCTORS
WHO HAVE TREATED ME
AT VARIOUS HOSPITALS
THESE PAST MONTHS

Thank you to Edwin Smet,
my (other) friends, family, and Sara –
and all my past and present animal friends,
especially Suetonius.

PREFACE

'Buddy I'm a kind of poet… and I have a lot of stories to tell' – to paraphrase a classic song that my dear friend Thor used to croon to me late at night, when we were young, and in our cups.

Those stories – and my many views on contemporary poetry, or the world we live in today (say, poetics to politics by way of polemics) – are not for this preface.

I will make one glum observation – I believe that the very meaning, purpose and value of poems have been lost for most people – the *what are they for*. If you don't know what a thing does, you're more likely to throw it away.

The poems I write may seem a bit traditional (or not), depending on who reads them, but they are composed with a strong belief in the value of poems as art and artifice.

I personally feel poems present a selected verbal moment that can be returned to – the balance between repeatability and originality is the same as with a popular song – every time you play it, it should be as good as the first time.

I spent Christmas 2021 in St Johns Wood in an ICU with a failing heart; and as of this date am being treated for this serious condition. Poems may or may not arise from this very frightening, sad and unexpected series of experiences, in future.

These are the poems that directly preceded this; the shadow of stress and illness (endemic in the world) may enter, but the theme is only incidentally, if at all, about the heart; or, perhaps, only about the heart.

T.S.
Maida Vale, February 18th, 2022

TABLE OF CONTENTS

THE DIG

My wife, Tegan and Sara are playing again,
And your name is Sara Egan, which I always think
Meant they're your band; and the sun is a bit out,
It's Friday. We're in a nightmare, a pop song,

And a pandemic. All at once, it's like popcorn
Mixed with blood, after a cinema slaughter.
It's like life was sad and generous, together,
Kind and vicious, and that's true, so true.

How many of my poems started with I do?
How many complained of marriage, like
It was a terminal wall? I feel dumb, small,
And insipid, now. I've been failing since

Conception, but my self-hate is not the point,
Or is, in a footnote sort of way. The point is,
The light today is the light of Eden, the light
Of when a man was impaled, the light when

That great ship was buried in Norwich,
The sun-catching gold of the helmet hidden
Beneath the ground so the ground could save
Its meaning, as any grave will do for anyone;

The light says, come out, spring is around,
Come out and play. The world is safer,
And longer, than you think. There are two worlds,
The one we have for a bit, and the other,

That thinks of eons, not mothers, fathers.
Nature is not a person, and is not in danger,
It is the danger, and it is the hour; it arrives,
Like a tidal wave across a village. All

We can do is listen to songs, funny-dance,
Make words talk, laugh, and watch news;
Death rises, falls, a graph that is an autograph
Of the most famous king that ever crossed

The land. A shadow is a ruler that never fails.
It ends briefly, playing a good game with the sun,
But the sun dies as often, and is less cunning;
We think we are blessed, but that is like running

Into the Irish sea and thinking, this is for us,
Even as it pulls back, roars forward into lungs;
Breathe while you can, say the usual lessons,
Keep acting like children, amused by cultural

Goodies, gentleness, cats and cream, tiny dogs;
It is levels, never less than many, moving fast;
We cannot haul the nets out; this ship not ours;
The prow breaks past ice, fire, air, and all furies

Know it for the earth itself, sailing the buried kingdom
Up out of the long grain, to reclaim what was fallow,
To surprise, with narrow blades, in definitive fashion,
Our lives of MRIs and surgery, endometriosis,

New pain, to take by force the daily prognosis,
Shake it like a fine tiger on a caught slower thing,
Shake the moment out of its sea lanes, into memory,
A violence as certain, cold, imperious, as a British museum.

April 16, 2021

CANADIAN THANKSGIVING 2021

An entirely unearned sense of unexpected ease
Comes this Sunday, perhaps because of the earlier
Raucous post-mask brunch at a table with seven others
Debating, rowdily, the British empire, how one manager's
Nursing home saw fifteen deaths in two weeks last year.
Over vegan crepes and flat whites, after exercising

In the park, amid rain, then sun, as a London October, this
Occurs; I am gently teased for publishing conservatives
But can any book deserve a bonfire,
Even as evil as *Kampf?* I try to justify the neutral stance
Assayed by publishers wanting to take no sides,
Yet it feels a poor excuse for indecision, I agree.

I am thankful for much this year even apart from survival,
And the lives of my loved ones who survived,
I am one of the most fortunate of those not famous, not lean,
I can give thanks also for the weather, and my God, who,
Whether or not I believe in them, either remains
Or was never present anyhow. And that's the muddling

Position in the road I am on; relatively powerless,
In the grand game of policy and airlifts, but so much more
Powerful than the wretched of the earth, the refugees
Who never seem welcomed, whose bodies *and* minds
Are unwanted, who do not represent good value,
Are not start-up quality, who we do not invest in.

And I am with sin and have the nightmares to wreck sleep,
But I do not cross the deep to source a stable land.
And yes, various worlds complain of imbalanced needs.
And we have been unable yet to inculcate our creeds,
So that they interleave our patterns of behaviour,
Because, being humanised animals, we expertly misuse

Our capacity to love, and to save each other, at sea.
And Thanksgiving was, it may be, a foul instance
Of settler hypocrisy, praising a benefactor for things
Taken for granted, stolen from others' soil; no
Burnt wick without first enflamed oil; the devil
Is in the forgetfulness before the industry and toil.

We neglect the other as we neglect the souls
We no longer seem to believe we have, we here
Being, I fear, only the common sense I can glean from talk,
The media, reading. And without a soul, without a respect
Of all widespread, strife-facing, endangered communities,
We must remain encamped, in ignoring forts, staving off

The wilderness in us we exploit
To be cold heartless conquerors,
That gets projected, like a Mercator map, to misshape
What the world out there is, or might be said to look like,
Which, being contested daily, is hard to see, really,
Let alone alter, let alone bear.

But we do know our little stockades
Are partial, are enclosed, and do not share the bountiful
Bounty of what is, in fact, spread out before us, to hand,
What can be uplifted, uprooted,
Drilled for, removed. The high natural we decline
To adore, in our tech-researched quest for artifice,

For what the next advance will be.
There is something, small,
That feels like presented, actual material –
A channel-wet child, that we can hold, if not secure,
Whose very encumbrance feels
About the same as a bar of solid gold.

THANKSGIVING, OCTOBER 2021

WHO CARES WHO THE NEXT JAMES BOND WILL BE?

My cat owns zero property, is a year zero creature, unshaped by much
More than breeding, instinct and how he's been cuddled since birth;
So even animals, then, are part of the set of objects controlled
By ideation's desiring hands, the caresses of want, supply,
And superfluous demand. Petrol is missing, anger soars, Volvos halt,
The army comes out, to deliver the gold dust that runs
The world; how will a universe without fossil fuels go?
I guess the battery kings will collude with the electricity kings,
Who will intermarry with the waterfall kings, and the wind kings,
And the electric cable kings, and the rare mineral kings,
And the kings who design five-time-faster than sound rockets,
And these will decide who gets the manuka honey, who fiscally
Owns the Labradors, the Persians, British Blues, Siamese,
The Pekinese, and all the wilder hybrid pets we will still call ours,

SEPTEMBER 28, 2021

NEW AUTUMN POEM

The requisite
Light tightening moment
Captured like in a Polaroid cliché
In the similarly overly-familiar poem,
Announcing the individual's sense of autumn
Coming in, presuming that a) people's experiences
Have value and b) those valuable experiences can be
Transferred in language and c) there's nothing more important
At the present time to occupy the reader's time, like the collapse
Of the ecological balance, or the imminent super-volcanic eruption,
Or the fact that almost all our communications are an uneasy matrix
Regulated poorly but brutally by the unequal dance between power, or
Power's desire to accrue power, and the underlying, ideologically structured
Rules of language itself, indeed, the very structures that define what a poem or
Language might be; so that, to pause, in mid-September, as it gets dark in a garden
In a privileged part of the former colonising hegemon, in the metropolis of London, to
Reflect on the sadness of fading light, inevitable ageing and death, the cat high in the tree...

TWO JULY POEMS

1.

I forget the July hammer
of sun each year building
my boat of wavering sleep
as heat swims on air
to reach a beached tree;
no crash of bird or rose
sinks this high hammock
sol makes just with itself;
only nature is artificer
enough to change a world
by degrees, as instant as
weather which is creation
of new terms to live on.
I drift for once with dry book
as a child aloft on poetry;
summer is its own genre,
shaded garden in a library
heart borrows from a shelf
then keeps forever forgotten;
parted early brightness years
the loan we can't return.

2.
Speaking to themselves
what we call flowers
what we see as colours
know their requirements
so act accordingly at night

and dawn, mid-summer
or when frost comes on;
nothing we say is meant
as rain to feed their stamens,
pistils, buds, or leaves; bright
petals lure in what needs
nectar, their vines explore
smart like the digital world;
connection is nature's word;
we learn the language of them
then arrogate our names for
their complete extensions of
baroque entanglements above
human orders or ideals of love.

JULY 19TH

I almost died
But so did you
The story is old
Before it is true

And when it's gone
It's gone for bad
So put out the bunting
And try to be glad

The empire of song
Is dancing away
The vessels are sinking
The birds have gone grey

The squares are deserted
Or maybe obscene
The windows are breaking
The sea is piss-green;

It's a time of regretting
And making new friends;
A time of renouncing
And making amends;

The words that went deeper
Are gasping for air;
The world that was better
Is not very fair;

What was so impressive
Is now dinky and mean;
We've grown better whiskers
And eat to be lean;

It's all very tragic
And slightly bizarre;
The epic is dying but
We'll fly in fast cars;

Delivery is billions
And content is queen;
But there's no reading
Of the in-between;

We live on the edge
Of extremes like two stars
Gaseous and distant
And brutally far;

I try to get closer
But truths cause a rift;
We're adrift on what's melting,
The soul needs a lift;

Identity spirals into the air;
It's good to be someone
Who can't be elsewhere;
You belong to your own self

And name it as such;
My own sex is nebular
And my love is a crutch
At a rubber plantation

In hateful Brazil;
The jungles are burning
And the moon is awhirl;
The decade is coming, it may

Already have, in which
Some of us are living
And the rest get to watch;
Or even more likely

And less pleasant-serene,
Some of us survive
For the rest to berate
On media not yet invented

But sure to communicate
Vast networks of vitriol
Which is as should be –
Some stand to attention,

Some take a knee,
But the plan is to transfer
What's good from who's not;
By means of what's brutal

In deed or in thought;
I am always frightened,
And usually on meds;
Afraid of the enemy, the bill

And the feds; the ones who
Chant slogans, the ones who deny
Reasons for complaining:
The pie in the sky, the tree

That's on fire, money that's bled;
I'm anxious with hawks, and with the reds.
I'm shot in the middle,
Like all who pretend, it's business

As usual when the world's not a friend,
But a series of maxims enlarged by a trend;
California is burning, Death Valley is hot;
The ice is not colder, it's rather not;

The weather is turning, it's gone berserk!
Since mankind devised things, the train
And the piston, the Jenny that twerks;
Who invents the engine is she who wins,

But only industrially, and not for all time;
For time is divided, like a Pullman line,
Some seats are plusher, some are sublime;
The current car we're in is plummeting fine,

Right off the cliff where the bend should have been;
We're that part of history
That's terminal rust; the blot on the ledger
The uncomfortable thrust;

It's hard to accept the future is post-human
And probably post-Earth; our brains
In the wiring, with bodily thirst;
It's all going to happen, it already did;

This poem's just a repeat of what once was hid.
This is the ending when you flip the switch.
It goes off, it comes on, there's even a bleep;
Enjoy rejuvenescence, bright from new sleep.

FOR G. HILL

The tense forfeited style
prepares its terse fortress

of integrity. Lesser canons
fire louder but expend

more hubris. Carefully
prepare the corpse

for resurrection with oils.
The miracle if

it occurs is minute precision.
God moves molehills

also, most of all. In droves.
After the greater flood.

POEM 3.1

Life is more precious-fragile
than even the icicle, turnstile;
the diamond and butterfly know:
roses grow to wither off all reds,

snow plummets to dirty up piles
like slaughtered infantry in mud;
god evolves so flies infect easier
as children enjoy gross tumours;

love is the wet-wounded horse
running through bullets to reach
their lost rider bleeding slowly in
a spring riverbed of new blood;

I need to pray for compassion
for those enduring the common
injuries of night or day on earth;
but cannot justify a virgin birth.

It is not sullied to be human
but it is to be attacked alone
circled by a rudderless army
spending their last ammunition.

THE STEAMSHIP

I can already see my life far behind me
Like that far puff of smoke the steamship leaves
And I see on the postcard blue, against the rails
Most of the books, doctors and lovers waving,

Before puffing out of existence like a dream
Being blown away by the morning. It's not sad,
But it feels like autumn, or the end of school,
It has a whiff of sadness, like a stolen kiss,

Like anything stolen is somewhat pitiful.
It's still mine, I suppose, that fading cloud,
But not mine to reach anymore, I am not a seabird,
Not yet, and likely never, unless it happens,

In which case I might fly somewhere else anyway.
I don't even want to risk jumping off the deck
And into the opal sea, not now. I am glad about
The books, the proof-reading, the coffee flirts,

The hassles of taking glasses off in airports
To be scanned. I admit as much, it was okay.
But now I am past those trailing puffs of white,
That were not ever glories, but daily exhalations,

And the ship has crossed an equator with me onboard.

THE BOOK

Wildness and order mingle in every bedroom
Among clothes, among sheets,

Along the length of thigh, the razor's
Neat blade, the incomplete pairs

Of knee-high socks – the tingle
Of recognition, when eyes meet,

Or almost meet. Princess, in the tent
In the desert, where you encamped,

Did they wait outside all night long,
As you lay there, perfected subject

Of desire, of high object's perfection?
Or did at least one of the kingdom's

Less noble ones enter the splendid dream
That is being among the chaos of passion,

The indescribable thrill of being wrong
Together with a second embodied mind,

When one corporeality finds another in the fury
Of entanglements that cry out for complex absolutes?

I think it happened, the abject wilderness
Entering civilisation, opposites inscribing

Their skin with the language of fulfilment,
Writing the book no one else can read.

NEW NOVEMBER

I like testing myself against November,
the month most likely
to get poets chattering about bare fingers
reaching for the sky; most poetry is a decision
rarely regretted, the litterer having
moved on. Yes, I just called poets messy;
or careless, like people in *Gatsby* or Maddox
Ford, or other Edwardian novels.
Time to take yourself less seriously chum,
drop the ideation we care when or where
you managed to pamper your bum-bum.
I see a world, it appears to exist even when
I am asleep – it swims in the deep
gulf between things we lose, we need to keep.
God once maintained the world, or never did;
now, it is a renegade, careening –
heat is neutral, all being equal, but that
is not the entropy we require for flourishing;
the levels here calibrated what could be,
to rudely shift a lever thrusts the kilter away;
November days like any charcoal
used to encourage industry, retain a coat
of grey that rarely if ever washes away;
they start melancholy, end that way,
like a listed, brick-black factory that once smelted,
whose purpose has melted away; levelling
goes in both directions, heaps or extracts.
The weather is a distraction; it is our super mac.
This season will not sign any agreement,
resolve a burning question, or endure; no
month is ever final cure for the spinning year.
Solutions may rinse out, like rain, in finer gradations.

SPILL RHINE

The only reason the first letter of these lines starts with a capital
Letter is because that's the way the computer formats it for me.
What has poetry done for you lately, my shrink
At the Montreal Jewish General Hospital asked (Kleenex box
Suitably on hand) as I lay on the sweat-stained little bed,

Like a twilight London sky bleeding out on a gurney.
Even Sabein was ignored after being fried by Freud,
Befriended young by Jung, spanked into conscious theory by men
Who went on to found the best way to get paid for bad dreams.
I apologise here to my mother for not being famous.

FOR THE UNSHORTLISTED

Other years. And the best
never win. Dickinson etc.
Plus, maybe lost in the post.

Or too political. Or less.
You deserve a hug. We love
your work. Eventually. Maybe.

In the end the tortoise...
Art is long, life far harder.
Hang in there. Most lose.

Just fashion. Judges. Marmite.
Don't let the bastards get you
down, mate. Try a novel next?

ON ARRIVING

Only when you leave the door
Do you get what you came for

The thrill of being persona non
For those who sing bad songs

Leave by the exit to escape
The matadors and their capes

Who only skewer a dying bull
Loving a bank when mostly full.

You cannot be actually radically
A writer if you tend to employ

As agent or attorney a brutalist
Fighter who does the business

With a bruised or bloody fist;
Unless you want on the shortlist

To claim to be all that's truth
Except when in a killing booth.

Choose your choices like words
They can end up making worlds.

HANDSOME MAN IN AUTUMN

walking past so surely, solid,
so tall, groomed, and suited,
maybe a model, exuding
a scent of permanence,
stability, old fashioned Cary
Grant comfort, shower with me,
be my daddy, hail cabs by
my side, make me handsome
too, comfortable in my hide;
I know I am outmodedly bi,
and stupidly naive to be
impressed by the outside
of your impression, your strong
stride, as if no hail of bullets
or complaint could restrain
your masculine credentials –
come right in, step inside,
take what you want, I cry
inwardly at your sham beauty,
a Potemkin savoir faire;
I don't care. I just want to die
having been your major domo.

THE PROBLEM FOR AN ATHEIST

is you can't disprove
what might exist:
it's true God may not be real,
but some believe they feel
a love in a mushed internal quantum.
The mess is in existence
where God could be said
to quirk, when not hushed dead.
God surpasses the personal
binaries and are in the space
where fiction and fact branch
out to flourish an expanding forestry
of what might or not ever be.
I almost live in that possibility.

LOVE'S MAD WHEN IT'S ALL GOOD.

When it's bad it's not itself.
Everyone falls, few climb, but
My heart's after too many stairs.
Take the waters of Baden Baden
For past affairs. Sights narrow,
Eyes still widen. Had, then
Hadn't, in the flights of time.
Love's best before fiscal
Decline: the slump that leads
Past collar crime to devaluation.
It's only insane because rhyme.
The exciting thrown back hood,
Perfection of a shared Abaddon.

PROGRESS

I have nothing to say
Except I am what is in the way.

How do I write without conquest?
Simple: stop and leave the paper to the rest.

POEM AS SIMPLE AS BREAD

I have only a few lines
to tell you what may be true
after all the cunning lies
of my beautiful thousand poems
treacherous as ice in spring.

HOMERIC

Troy is burning.
The soldiers stand around,
looking at their swords
on the ground, like seashells.
The barbarians have almost
won; they are spearing
captured citizens
like fish. It is a sight
displeasing to the gods.
Why don't they defend
their city? Zeus thunders.
The silence answers.
The fire answers. What
is the purpose of war
having surrendered once
before? Defeat can feel
like fate. Or a tipping wave.
Without fighting we are lost,
the gods say. And they are.

MICHAEL LONGLEY

Flower master, the classics
are like butterflies to you
that gather on your gentians
and hydrangeas, the poppies
of war fields past and to come.
Your home is where sky is,
and land, wine-sea. Your plough
turns lost sod over for new
growing; a blade that cuts
soil has not yet touched skin.
Poems can look delicate,
even slight, but be long resilient
under snow. Your perennial
words work this knowing.

I CAST A POEM ON THE WATER

I cast a poem on the water
for all the birds to stir;
once these poems were
my food and shelter;
the birds indifferently look
but never devour this scatter;
for them bread is better
and easier to read than book;
no one can master
another's need or create
more than the plate
on which they feed;
art is not what animals favour;
art is still a poet's only flavour.

FREEDOM

ideologies offer few rewards:
a world of cruelty from liberty

or intolerable equality by sword
means either soul or body free.

I NOW KNOW

my father is alive
in the same way

that Marcus Aurelius,
the calm Caesar is also;

quality not duration the truth;
each existence pertains,

hits a note, lasts a time,
is music as music is

rhyme; you are in a slice
like a tree ring, a sampled

plug of ancient informing ice;
I am in it as it fades, owning

a bit of rippling radiation going;
movement is not all; staying

behind is what records contain.
We are truly resonant remains;

this clustering is fine, mine;
the fur of my beloved feline

shares this brief sign we make;
a thin line on a graph rising

like purrs only to decline;
but it stains, there's the thing.

WHEN I TOOK FROM MY NEIGHBOUR

he thanked me for his hunger;
when I built her a new wall
she smiled at my good humour;
when I planted his fields myself

he donated his own plough;
when I moved in to their house
she offered me her good towel;
I am large because not as small;

power becomes an excuse;
history is from worse to here:
I present you with gentle bombs
that build by the psalms, tombs.

SOMETIMES I AM OTHER TIMES

off like when the head goes a little bit away
from itself, and I go that ways often,
soft sort of the world can skew,
like when you're told by someone
you love of the blood test, and a wide gulf
between before and fear grows too fast
like you know what does and I am afraid
for skin that feels and skin inside
that must be gone
like a bad rumour or vicious spy.

2.
Editing poems for this book
I can see the dividing line,
A break, between then, before
And this time here.
Time is a kind of name.
All the I *times* in these lines
Were never really here, or there,
After all. It's not planned,
To heart fail.

TODD SWIFT

CIRQUE

I once dated a circus freak's
daughter and it is no business
of yours how he pulled nine

nine-inch rusty nails out of each
nostril nonchalantly over
pasta dinner at his house, and

neither is it anything to do
with you that he let me stay
over with her on the bed of

nails in their basement; nor
should you care that she was
a bearded fat lady and I,

I walked across red coals to be
her one and only dog-faced boy.

POEM AS NOVEL

i have written every poem
like a novel, but readers, at least
some, mistake duration for
quality, thinking a thick stack
of glued together paper is more
complex than one page pared
down, like a razored prisoner
whose shocking skull speaks
vividly of each vile dull crime;
do you prefer pearl or ocean?
sorbet or feast? chaste kiss
or harem? less is often deeper;
one prayer screams bibles,
you fall once when you sleep,
one confession can cure all sin.

POEM AS SYRUP

i now know where everything
i need to do resists silence:
a Quebec ski lodge in winter,
converted into a family home

but keeping the check-in desk
so all my cousins and i could
ring the bell, sign the register;
of books, cats, outer snowing

i can sing, this source of mine,
this thing called once upon;
among still maples and birches
time drips like sap into buckets,

collecting for the syrup sleigh;
later boiled in a vat big as loss,
so sweet, thick, slow, staying
to pour on what's boiled away.

UNBEARABLE, BEAR IT LIKE A TREE

has climbers, not a storm;
storms last their expression;
departing are just work to do;
the hospital has grass outside;
we know what leads the band,
a tossing pride marching on;
not so noticed is a final player;
the last music is heard more;
darkness is a candle unlit, go
from there; throw matches
at a window showing oblivion;
i bring you a middle day,
after birth, before failure;
play in that part of time a bit.

IMPERIAL BEDROOMS

beyond blame or guilt
lie the house and gardens
majestic power built
the upholstered chair

inlaid with gold
in which sat the conqueror
who defeated an emperor
to wear a diamond star

on a blue sash
mined from old empires
set on fire to build in ash
and dragons or swans

to adorn wrought iron
or ecstatic plants, walled
lands set alight by seed
to flower beauty carefully

under silver lock and cobalt key.

POEM AS CONVOCATION

Know what was said at Thebes,
in Athens and up in calm Tibet:
what hasn't happened has yet
to slinky down back stairs
to fix itself a midnight sandwich
of fear, hope and naive devotions.
The stars are eventual coals
gone the other way from blazons.
We slip into
that nook of life that's brief;
seeking interminable kind relief.
Forgive enemies and bow low.
The endless *If* may still know.

I WAKE UP

I take seriously what I do to say
poems as objects that arise
from compromised humanity;
never claim to speak for you.

THE EDGE OF THE FOREST

is where theory goes
after knowledge goes
after skill goes
after the body goes
after the light goes
after the animals go
after the wind goes
after the spirit goes
after hunting goes
after the mind goes
after the will has gone
after terror has gone
as history goes
as night weather goes
as lies go
as the natural has gone
as dying goes
the gods have gone
God goes as God
into that forest

ANYONE ELSE

like me feel they're slipping
up like a slippery slope
or soap on a short rope,
tipping over like a valise
in a windy old aerodrome
stamped all over with Toledo,
Marrakech and Home
or Bust? I do the vertigo
dance very well, I do,
the banana peels plus ice
beneath the balls of my feet
skedaddling oiled marbles
atop a maniacally flapping
parakeet cawing *Anne Heche*!

I SEE NOW THE WAY IS TO

not have to have that I there
at all, not really. Language
is in the way of the Word

in the same way that time
is the opposite of infinity.
It gets spiritually messy now –

poems with wisdom become
embarrassing like promises
to return a book. We know a lie

when we hear a lie pal.
The truth is shy or it is not.
Let's sidle up to the shadow

of the edge of the sort of bit
that whispers like a hole
in a water-bucket. Listen

it never says. It doesn't need
to claim a spot on the show.
Roll up the maps. You're here.

Ludicrous but arrival's fast.
Good is god with an extra zero.
Speed is light. This is lighter.

I think you're going to need
a smaller boat. Your soul
is the size of the moment before

there were any moments.
Yes we were all angels on a pin.
Not really. Those are symbols

for a rushing so complete
stillness is the best travel.
We're in the middle of the sun.

We're bigger than begun.
Peace be with you. War also.
This sort of idea is a mixed bag.

You are the foal and the nag,
the halter, rider and throw.
You are the window and snow.

The space between a and o.
Now go and tell yourself
the glad news. Naively.

No need to believe or join.
The corner comes to itself
naturally like I am a Mayan

and the restless iguana, a battery
discovered in England
and a flat screen off until.

HERE WE GO AGAIN IS TOO GLUM,

but after the cortisol's burnt
off, it's a physical reaction

to another nose-dive time,
bus terminal of waiting to sicken

or just get bored; the Uricon
gone, the Roman yeoman's

skull is ash; Omicron arrives
a bad sequel, rude invasion;

troubles too soon; our plans
human-inconsequential. Law

can't kill Darwin's variant
born dominant over Delta;

it feels like free fall, cancelled
Christmastime; worse to come.

IF I SAY I AM SCARED I LIE, SCAR

tissue on my fear hardens care;
but I am on dead-eyed alert

for what collapses eventually
after too long tired, albeit fortified.

WHEN I SAY I AM HAVING A TOUGH TIME

i mean we are all having a tough time
by which i mean a contiguous line
drawn from the me that is unreal
to the communal you that remains

unproven. Still 38 years ago
at the party at Johnny Prince's
by the fireplace i should have kissed
them instead of taking laughing gas;

which is why my PhD was on
F.T. Prince who at Oxford
hesitated in his desires also.

MY LIFE'S NOT DIFFICULT

that's rude to the drowned
crossing from Charybdis
to the UK's Scylla – across
the Straits – not Messina
but the Channel – and not via
the Chunnel... but also crude
to deny a whirlpool is a mind
foundering, unbuilt – the Medusa
wreck or Deutschland – thought
curled round itself corkscrew style;
I own ruins inside. Please aid
those abandoned at sea,
those lost on dry land.

UNTITLED

it doesn't matter that
  no one is
    listening
that 'no one'
     is drilling
a hole straight through
      the universe
powered
  only
       by
   your   poems

OCTOBER 2021

The words go on.
The words go on.
Do they now?
And how?
Slow?
It is autumn,
time of dead poets
in Ireland.
Time of dead poets.
Go on. Go on.
Poets have words.
They are still listening.
Hear all the language.
Trees of it,
doing everything.

LISTENING TO FLEET FOXES SING

a few days before Christmas,
after two years not resolving
our fears, of universal dread
normal now though it ruins
what came before, up ahead
also; I recognise a despoiled
gentleness, a carapace soul;
touch less, hold less, colder;
survival mode but unable
to go careful among your
sacred vessels, valued tombs.
I am a thuggee, boxed numb
to intimacy, supplication, balm.
Christ, bring back tenderness.
My abandoned heart appalling.

POET'S BIOGRAPHY

Todd Swift was born in Montreal, Quebec, in 1966 on Good Friday.

From an early age he composed stories and poems, and gave speeches, becoming first the provincial high school debating champion, then a top international speaker at university. In his 20s, after graduating from Marianopolis and Concordia, he wrote over a hundred hours of TV for the CBC, Hanna-Barbera, Disney, Fox, and HBO, among others. He was a story editor for *Sailor Moon*. In his 30s he met his wife to be, and moved with her to Budapest, then Paris, then London. In the UK he took an MA and PhD from UEA.

He has been a university lecturer, a visiting scholar at Cambridge (Pembroke College), and for ten years, the director of Eyewear Publishing, now BSPG. He was written and had published over 500 poems; and has edited a dozen anthologies, and hundreds of pamphlets and books for others. He has hosted, for over 30 years, countless cabarets, launches, readings, and other literary events, not least the Oxfam series, and the New McGill series, with Bill Furey.

He has a brother, Jordan, and a godson, Alex; loves cats and animals in general, and is married to an Irish lawyer, Sara. He is now British-Canadian and converted from Anglicanism to Catholicism about a decade ago. He struggles often with his faith, and like Verlaine, Baudelaire, and Jung, is fascinated by the duality of the human psyche. In December 2021 he was diagnosed with Heart Failure.

Lightning Source UK Ltd.
Milton Keynes UK
UKHW041314240322
400557UK00001B/27